IMAGES OF ENGLAND

Chingford

IMAGES OF ENGLAND

Chingford

Stephen Pewsey

NONSUCH

This book is dedicated to John Boyes,
President of the Chingford Historical Society

First published 1996
This new pocket edition 2005
Images unchanged from first edition

Nonsuch Publishing Limited
The Mill, Brimscombe Port,
Stroud, Gloucestershire, GL5 2QG
www.nonsuch-publishing.com

British Library Cataloguing in Publication Data.
A catalogue record for this book is available from the British Library.

ISBN 1-84588-140-0

Typesetting and origination by Nonsuch Publishing Limited
Printed in Great Britain by Oaklands Book Services Limited

Contents

Acknowledgements

I would like to thank the staff of Vestry House Museum, in particular Nigel Sadler, for all their help and for permission from them and the Chingford Historical Society, whose collection is held by the Museum, to use the photographs in this volume. Over half of the images in the book have been drawn from these collections. High quality copies of these photographs can be obtained from:

Nigel Sadler
c/o Vestry House Museum,
Vestry Road,
Walthamstow
E17 9NH
Tel: 020 8509 1979

Other images are from the Eclipse Archive.
Thanks also to my wife, Paulette, for all her technical assistance.

Introduction

'Chingford is entitled to be ranked with the most pleasant of our Essex villages' wrote the historian D.W. Coller in 1861 in his *People's History of Essex*. The parish stands in south-west Essex, the River Lea forming its western edge and the boundary with Middlesex. To the east is the little River Ching, hardly more than a brook, and to the north, the open expanse of Chingford Plain and Epping Forest beyond, while in the south, Chingford merges imperceptibly with its neighbour, Walthamstow.

There is surprisingly little evidence for early settlement, but Chingford seems to have begun life as a small Saxon hamlet beside the Lea where traffic now roars over the North Circular bridge. Here was once the cëgingaford, the 'dwellers by the stumpy ford'. In medieval times, Chingford was a small and unremarkable parish, comprising a number of isolated 'ends' in typical Essex fashion, including Chingford Green and Chingford Hatch. Chingford was divided into two manors by the time of the Norman Conquest; Chingford Earls and Chingford St Paul's (so named from their erstwhile owners, the Earl of Essex and St Paul's Cathedral), and before the Industrial Revolution life in Chingford would have revolved round the unchanging agricultural cycle on these two manors and other scattered farms.

Epping Forest, earlier known as the Forest of Essex and Waltham Forest was an important local feature, as the whole of the parish fell within the bounds of Forest Law, and the actual wooded area in the north was used for feeding pigs, and of course for its timber resource, not to mention game. The low-lying marshes beside the Lea were also important as sheep-pasture, and the Lea itself abounded with fish. Agriculture thus dominated local life, though there was some tile-making and brick-making too. Hunting was an important pastime for the aristocracy, and Chingford is fortunate to possess within its boundaries the remarkable 'Queen Elizabeth's Hunting Lodge', a grandstand built by Henry VIII, recently magnificently restored.

The arrival of the railway in 1873 changed the face of Chingford and ended its rural isolation. Development began slowly around Chingford Green and by 1881 the population was still only 1,387. The passing of the Epping Forest Act in 1878, and the subsequent opening of Epping Forest to the public in 1882 caused many changes in Chingford. Queen Victoria's arrival at Chingford station and her subequent grand procession to declare the forest open were long remembered locally. The hordes of East Enders and other visitors pouring into the Forest at weekends and Bank Holidays made Chingford something of an inland tourist resort, its residents turning their hands to entertaining the visitors with refreshments, funfairs and side-shows.

Chingford became a municipal borough in 1894. Its population had quadrupled by 1901, though it was still less than 5,000, and most development took place after the First World War. Because of this late development, Chingford was fortunate to have retained many green and open spaces, and to have a much lower housing density than its neighbours. As such it was, and to some extent remains, a sought-after dormitory town. Municipal borough status was granted in 1938 as Chingford's population had risen to about 25,000. Although mainly residential, a strip of land along the North Circular Road was developed for light industrial activity, and is now being transformed from industrial park to retail park, as so often happens.

Major housing development after the war included the Friday Hill estate, built by the London County Council out of the Heathcote lands which had been held by that family since 1774. There has also of course been much infill and a certain amount of what might be called overdevelopment, as the pressure on land has grown. Despite the advent of the out-of-town shopping mall, Chingford remains important as a shopping centre, and the bustling parades along Station Road and Chingford Mount Road attract custom from far and wide, attractive for their variety and old-fashioned personal service. More recently, through its association with Norman (later Lord) Tebbit, the area's MP, the town was seen by some commentators to epitomise the spirit of that much-maligned creature 'Essex Man' – no-nonsense and enterprising. It was also claimed in the early 1990s to be the most expensive place to live in Britain!

In 1965, Chingford was joined to Walthamstow and Leyton to form part of the London Borough of Waltham Forest, thus breaking a thousand-year link with the county of Essex. Despite its 'London Borough' status and its closeness to London, Chingford still has many of the hallmarks of an Essex country town; a thriving social life ranging from amateur dramatics to allotment clubs, a loyalty to the neighbourhood and a sense of belonging, and the closeness of the forest bringing a whiff of rustic charm to even the busiest streets.

One

Chingford Green
and North Chingford

The western end of Chingford Green, c. 1890. A rustic scene, dominated by the spire of St Peter and St Paul, with the village pond, filled in in 1896, in the foreground. The village lock-up or 'cage' once stood beside this pond.

Despite the arrival of the railway in 1873, Chingford remained a pleasantly rural village for some decades; idyllic postcards like this were produced in large numbers for day-trippers visiting the Forest.

St Peter and St Paul, Chingford Green. This prominent Chingford Green landmark was built in 1844, to a Gothic design by Lewis Vulliamy, with striking alternate bands of yellow brick and black flint. The church was needed as the original parish church (All Saints on Chingford Mount) was becoming more and more isolated and ruinous as the population moved northward.

Interior of St Peter and St Paul. The church features a number of items taken from All Saints, including the twelfth-century font and eighteenth-century pulpit. The chancel was massively extended in 1903.

Green Farm. This reminder of Chingford's agricultural past once stood on the north side of Chingford Green, on the site of the present-day North Chingford library.

The Lodge, Chingford Green, c. 1905. Chingford became a moderately fashionable retreat for City businessmen in the eighteenth and nineteenth centuries, and a number of fine houses were built in the parish (though few survive). The Lodge, built around 1890, was later divided into two tenements.

The Catholic church of Our Lady of Grace and St Teresa. One of the more recent additions to Chingford Green, this building sits directly opposite St Peter and St Paul, occupying the prominent site on the corner of Station Road and Kings Road. Founded in 1919, the present building dates from 1931, with an adjacent Roman Catholic school founded in 1934.

The original Bull & Crown, which stood behind the site of the present building. The shop next door was jokingly referred to by locals as 'Chingford Town Hall'. The pub was once known as the Bull's Head.

Another view of the old Bull & Crown. The pub stood in Bull Lane, renamed Kings Road in 1901 in honour of King Edward VII.

The Bull & Crown, built in 1899 in an astonishingly flamboyant and florid style, described by one archtiectural observer as 'Edwardian pomposity...in the wildest Loire style'.

After a short spell with an imposed 'modern' name, the Bull & Crown has now quite rightly had its historic name restored, much to the satisfaction of local residents.

Carbis Cottage. This early nineteenth-century weatherboarded cottage still stands on
Chingford Green.

King's Head Hill Chingford.

The King's Head stands at the top of King's Head Hill, overlooking the Lea valley. The pub dates
back to at least 1787. This view, showing the police station to the right, dates from around 1916.

A horse and cart trots up the hill towards the King's Head in this undated postcard.

Chingford police station. Chingford formed part of the Metropolitan Police area since 1839, and this imposing building formed a Chingford Green landmark until replaced by a new station in 1975-7.

The arrival of the railway in 1873 marked a change in Chingford's destiny. A direct and convenient route into London encouraged both suburban development and opened up the forest for East End day-trippers. This photo shows Chingford's first station, which stood in King's Road (then called Bull Lane).

Chingford station. In 1878 the terminus was moved north to Maddox Lane, now Station Road, and the original station became a goods station. Plans to push the line up to High Beach were abandoned in the face of public opposition to further encroachments on the Forest.

Station Road quickly became an important axis, with shops and numerous cafes and restaurants. In this 1960s view, a No. 102 is seen in Station Road on the final leg of its journey from Muswell Hill.

Station Road, 1960s, looking east from outside the station.

There is some evidence of a postal-receiving house in Chingford as early as 1794. The earliest post office in the modern sense was the Tomalin family's cottage atop King's Head Hill. From 1887 until 1970 the post office was at 55 Station Road; this new building being opened in that year on the site of the old sorting office at 104 Station Road.

Chingford's War Memorial, which stands on the corner of The Ridgeway and King's Head Hill, was unveiled in 1921 by Lord Lambourne. Two hundred and forty of Chingford's young men did not return from the trenches.

Ridgeway House, typical of the large late Victorian and Edwardian houses which began to spring up in Chingford following the arrival of the railway.

Chingford Town Hall, The Ridgeway. Chingford became an Urban District in 1894, and a Municipal Borough in 1936. The Town Hall was opened in 1929.

Chingford's Coat of Arms. The stag's head symbolises the forest, and the wavy line represents the ford across the Lea from which Chingford takes its name. In 1965 Chingford became part of the London Borough of Waltham Forest.

Opposite above: Despite suburban growth, much of Chingford retained a rural aspect within living memory. This view shows The Ridgeway in 1930 looking east, from the junction with Mansfield Hill.

Opposite below: Another view of the Ridgeway; land has been fenced off ready for development.

The Ridgeway. 1930.

Mornington School. This small building on Chingford Green once housed a private school where, it was claimed, the staff made 'a feature of giving young pupils a thorough groundwork, and good discipline is combined with a happy and friendly atmosphere'.

Mornington Hall. When the school closed, the building was later used as a public hall.

Chingford, in keeping with its reputation as a high-class suburb, supported numerous small private schools. Normanhurst School is still thriving.

Melford House School advert, 1935. Note the proud boast: WIRELESS INSTALLED!

In 1931, Chingford Collegiate School was based in the Wesley Hall, Station Road, but
by 1935 it had found permanent accommodation in Warren Road.

St Egbert's College was a Roman Catholic school, founded in 1920 by the Brothers of
Mercy.

Chingford Green in the 1950s.

Station Road has been North Chingford's main shopping thoroughfare for over a hundred years.
This view dates from the turn of the nineteenth century.

One of the oldest established firms in Station Road is Uglow's fabric and furnishing store, founded by Frank Uglow in 1910, and now trading from 26-30 Station Road. This photo dates from the 1920s.

Telephone Chingford **65.**

F. E. UGLOW

General & Fancy Draper.

Everything for Ladies' and Children's Wear.

Chilprufe Underwear.
Abdo and Kingsonia Corsets.
Jaeger Goods.
Aza and Viyella Flannels.

Damask Cloths, Sheets and Household Linens.

37, STATION ROAD, CHINGFORD.

A 1923 advert for Uglow's.

A wide variety of shops offer a range of goods in Station Road. This 1923 advert is
for Huck's Pharmacy...

...while Miss Pudney's 'Art Needlework and Wool Repository' is seen here in this
ornate 1921 advert.

Station Road in 1917.

E. M. Phillips

HIGH-CLASS

𝔄rt & Church Needleworker.

SPECIALITIES : Coats of Arms, Private Crests, School and Club Badges embroidered. Ladies own work carefully and artistically mounted. Church materials of every description.

A LARGE VARIETY OF WOOLS, SILKS, ETC., STOCKED.

AGENT for Pearsalls Silks and Deightons Transfers.

———————

THE NEEDLECRAFT, 50 STATION ROAD, CHINGFORD.

Miss Pudney's shop had a rival in Phillips 'High-Class Art & Church Needleworker'.

RAWLINGS' MODEL STORE.

SPECIALITIES:

Butter : Bacon : Tea.

A Trial Solicited. Personal Attention to all Orders. No long **waits**, no short **weights**. Orders called for and delivered.

4, Station Road, CHINGFORD.

THE HOUSE OF QUALITY.

Rawlings' Model Store, a grocers, claimed 'No long waits, no short weights' in their punning advert.

A spectacularly patriotic shop window at Watkin's bakery, for Empire Shopping Week, 1931.

Station Road in 1923.

The same view in the 1960s. Brimble's bookshop can be seen at No. 62; James Brimble was a well-known local historian and expert on Epping Forest.

Banks' butchers, 73 Station Road, put on this fine seasonal display for Christmas 1975.

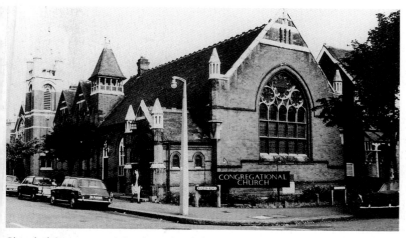

Chingford Congregational church was founded in 1888, an iron church being erected the following year. The adjacent Spicer Hall (named after the church's main benefactor, James Spicer), was opened in 1890, and in 1910 the iron church was replaced by the brick church seen in this view.

Left: Mount Echo Cottage in 1957. The Mount Echo farm occupied the triangle of land now bounded by The Ridgeway, Kings Head Hill, and Mansfield Hill.

Below: An unusual incident! A de Havilland DH6 crashed onto nurseries in Kings Head Hill in 1918 after taking off from nearby Chingford Aerodrome (now beneath the William Girling reservoir).

Two

Chingford
and the Forest

The whole of Chingford was within the Forest of Essex, which does not mean that it was entirely wooded but that the jurisdiction of forest law (such as royal hunting rights) encompassed the entire parish. The arrival of the railway and the opening of the Forest to the public in 1882 brought huge swarms of visitors to Chingford to admire lovely views like that seen in this postcard.

Despite determined efforts by landowners to enclose and develop the forest, many magnificent old trees survived, such as Grimston's Oak, which stands in a clearing north of Connaught Water.

Queen Elizabeth's Hunting Lodge. According to tradition, Good Queen Bess rode her horse up the stairs of this magnificent old building, but in fact, it was not built by Queen Elizabeth nor is it strictly a hunting lodge. Rather it is the larger of two 'standinges' or grandstands built by Herny VIII in the 1540s. The structure originally had open sides so that pot-shots could be taken by royalty and the assembled nobles at deer and other game driven out of the forest and towards the building.

The Hunting Lodge is therefore one of the oldest buildings in Chingford, though it has undergone considerable changes in its history. After centuries as a farmhouse, it was opened to the public in 1895 as the Epping Forest Museum, run by the Essex Field Club. This view shows the top floor gallery, shortly after its conversion to museum use.

Left: Chingford cattle mark. One of the rights enjoyed by those living in Forest parishes was the right to graze cattle within Forest land. To prevent straying, cattle were branded with a mark distinctive to each parish; Chingford's emblem was a crowned 'C'.

Below: By the middle of the nineteenth century, much of Epping Forest was under threat. Landlords were enclosing large chunks of it and converting the forest to farmland or developing it for housing. It was only after a long campaign, in which the villagers of neighbouring Loughton put up a stalwart defence of their ancient rights, and a series of court cases, that the Epping Forest Act was passed in 1878, with the Corporation of London being given the duty of conserving the Forest. Queen Victoria visited the Forest in 1882 to declare it open to the public; her arrival at Chingford station was greeted by immense crowds. This wooden archway was erected in her honour.

Forest Hotel, Chingford

Above: Royal Forest Hotel. Once the Forest was opened to the public, large numbers of tea gardens, public houses and other places of refreshment sprang up to cater for the hordes of visitors who descended on the area. The Forest Hotel, opened in 1890 and set in an imposing position on Dannett's Hill, was the largest inn in the district. Queen Elizabeth's Hunting Lodge can be seen in the distance on the right, partly behind the hotel coach-house.

Right: The imposing frontage of the Royal Forest Hotel, seen here in 1903, was originally four storeys high, but after a disastrous fire in 1912, it was not rebuilt to its full height.

Pole Hill. The obelisk was set up in 1824 to mark the original line of the Greenwich Meridian. However, in 1884, the meridian line was re-calibrated and found to lie 19ft west of the Pole Hill marker. Because of the spear shaped finial, the obelisk soon became identified in local legend as the site of one of the battles of Boudica (Queen Boadicea).

Pole Hill. A peaceful scene. At 300ft, this is the highest point in Chingford, and on a clear day there are spectacular views. The name derives from St Paul's, which formerly owned one of the two ancient manors of Chingford.

During the First World War, Pole Hill was the site of an anti-aircraft gun.

The gun crew was billeted in these adjacent huts; note the aircraft painted on the sides of the huts, used in identification training lessons.

Above: Pole Hill is perhaps best known for its association with T.E. Lawrence, Lawrence of Arabia. Lawrence's close friend Vyvyan Richards had a hut-like 'retreat' on Pole Hill since 1912, but in 1921 it was rebuilt when Lawrence bought fifteen acres of land on the hill. Lawrence frequently visited the wooden buildings seen in this photo and hoped ultimately to live on the hill. But, in 1929, he sold the land to Chingford Council, who returned it to the Forest and it was opened to the public in 1932.

Left: To the south of the Hunting Lodge is Warren Wood, and within the wood, Warren Pond, a scenic spot attracting many visitors.

Connaught Waters. This lake was originally a marshy area, dug out to form a lake in 1881 and extended in 1893, and named after the Duke of Connaught, appointed Forest Ranger in 1882. The popular beauty spot actually lies just across the Chingford border.

Butler's Retreat. Numerous 'retreats' were built throughout the Forest after 1882, some fairly modest tea-rooms while others were full-scale funfairs. Butler's Retreat was opened in 1891 in the barn of Queen Elizabeth's Hunting Lodge, and is still serving Forest visitors to this day.

The place of material interest in North Chingford is the—

CORONET CAFÉ

where high-class Refreshments are served at very moderate prices.

Accommodation for Parties, Receptions, Socials, Whist Drives, etc.—with a good aspect facing the Golf Course and Forest.

1 FOREST AVENUE
(CORNER OF BERESFORD ROAD)

2 Minutes from Station.   Bus Services 602, 38E & 145 pass the door.

Left: Many other eating establishments sprang up in Chingford to cater for trippers. In 1895 there were eleven tea gardens in the Urban District and a large number of cafes and pubs. The Coronet Café stood at No.1 Forest Avenue...

Below: ...but was later converted into a private house.

Opposite: Chingford Plain. This is Chingford's largest open space, and forms the southern edge of the Forest. However, by the mid-nineteenth century, the whole of the Plain had been taken over for arable farming, and it was not until the Epping Forest Act of 1878 that the area was restored to wilderness.

Robin Hoods Cabin. Chingford.

Above: Hawkwood House, *c.* 1910. This large house was built in about 1850 by Richard Hodgson, one of the chief figures behind the Victorian destruction of the Forest. He was one of the landowners who enclosed Chingford Plain and converted it into farmland, and he also cut down most of the ancient Hawk Wood which lay around his property. After Hodgson's death, the estate was bought on behalf of the City of London Corporation. During the Second World War it was temporary home to Chingford County High School, but the building was demolished after the war.

Left: Postcards can be misleading! This view of 'Robin Hood's Cabin' apparently shows a pleasant Forest scene in Chingford, but the building shown was actually the Swiss Cottage, which stood in Bush Wood, Wanstead, some miles away!

Three

Chingford at Work

A reminder of just how rural Chingford once was. This reaper-binder is working at Carrol's Farm, Sewardstone.

Poulter's Dairy, Chingford Hatch, c. 1936. Old Farm, which stood on Friday Hill, and may have once been an inn, has long been demolished.

Opposite above: The old village smithy – seen here, c. 1885 – stood on the green opposite the present-day site of North Chingford library.

Opposite below: Horse-drawn transport required not only a large infrastructure of blacksmiths, ostlers, sadlers etc., but also carters and wheelwrights. Jessops' wheelwrights shop in Chingford Hatch was still active in the 1930s. The workshop stood at the rear of these buildings.

Left: Roper's Farm, Larkshall Road, July 1970. Better known as Inks Green Farm. The Roper family were well known locally, and are commemorated in nearby Ropers Avenue.

Below: Bartrip's Coal and Coke Depot; this timber-framed cottage faced Chingford Green, on the site of the Catholic church.

Opposite above: A woman's work is never done! The kitchen range in Gomme's Farm, which stood at the top of Church Hill.

Opposite below: Electricity brought an end to much domestic drudgery. The North Metropolitan Electric Power Supply operated from 1900 in Waltham Abbey, Chingford and Walthamstow, but only began to provide power for private houses from 1923. This advert dates from 1927.

Chingford's many laundries provided a socially acceptable form of wage-earning work for the village women. This advertisement dates from 1923.

Nash's Laundry, also known as Chingford Laundry, was one of the oldest established laundries in the parish. It was situated on the Green, next to almshouses, dating from 1857 (with additions in 1887).

Westcott's Laundry was one of the better-known establishments in South Chingford.

A splendid Leyland fire tender from the inter-war years. Chingford had a volunteer fire brigade from around 1895, but was later covered by the services of the Essex County Fire Brigade.

Above: As horse transport gave way to the car, new companies sprang up to deal with the new demands of a motoring public. The Beechwood Engineering and Coach Plating Co., seen here in 1930, stood in The Ridgeway.

Left: Some larger industrial concerns were concentrated in the south-west of the district, along the North Circular Road, notably the works of the London Rubber Company, one of the world's largest producers of condoms.

Opposite above: The railway had opened up Chingford for development and tourism, and so was of considerable economic importance to the town. According to the 1891 census, twenty-four people worked for the Great Eastern Railway at Chingford. This view, a cobweb of gantries and sidings, dates from shortly after electrification of the line in 1960.

Opposite below: Another view, showing the signal box.

CIVIL DEFENCE

needs **YOU** now

If the Hydrogen Bomb were to be used on this country, there would be thousands of survivors who could be saved by **trained** Civil Defence workers.

There are five Sections in the Civil Defence Corps — Headquarters, Ambulance and First Aid, Rescue, Warden, and Welfare. Chingford needs volunteers to train in all Sections — men and women are equally welcome.

Full details from :

The Civil Defence Officer

Town Hall, Chingford

Telephone : SILverthorn 3601

16

Community-spirited individuals could always join the Civil Defence corps, as seen in this 1950s advert, though with hindsight it seems unlikely that much of Chingford would have survived a hydrogen bomb attack.

Four

Chingford at Play

Hunting was traditionally a popular sport within the Forest, notably the riotous annual Easter Hunt which always attracted large crowds. The Epping Forest Stag Hunt was a rather more select affair however. From 1798–1806 the staghounds were kenneled at William Mellish's house on Chingford Green.

Funfairs on Chingford Plain attracted huge crowds, and remain a regular seasonal attraction. From 1882 onwards, there were large numbers of attractions and sideshows to help part trippers from their money. The peak year was 1920 when, on Whit Monday, 100,000 arrived at Chingford station; trains ran every five minutes to cope with the crowds. Somerset Maugham set part of his 1897 story *Liza of Lambeth* at Chingford Fair.

Some of the sideshows can be seen in this engraving; boat-swings, donkey races and coconut shies.

The various Forest 'retreats' were immesely popular. John Riggs first had the idea of network of temperance tea-rooms providing refreshments for Forest visitors, and his first, opened in 1879, was the Chingford Retreat, though it is actually just across the border in Buckhurst Hill, in Brook Road.

Above: This 1899 advert shows the Jubilee Retreat, opened in 1887 on Hawkwood Farm, Bury Road. Jubilee Retreat was closed during the Second World War and refugees were billeted there. The site was later converted into flats and sports pavilions.

Left: One of the most spectacular attractions at the Jubilee Retreat was this huge helter-skelter. Other side shows included a steam-driven 'galloper' (i.e. a roundabout), swings, and pony and donkey rides.

Opposite above: Rigg's Retreat in Brook Road was renamed Langford's Retreat following rebuilding after a disastrous fire in 1905. Despite further fires, two world wars and economic difficulties, the tea-rooms at least continued in operation until as recently as 1969. It is now a caravan site.

Opposite below: The Royal Forest Hotel has already been mentioned, and still stands to this day, though now only three storeys high and without the ornate wrought-iron arcading. The building has recently been comprehensively refurbished by the new owners, Brewers Fayre.

LANGFORD'S RETREAT
(Late Riggs)   'Phone : Buckhurst **0465.**

Brook Road,
Buckhurst Hill.

Noted
Resort
for
Luncheons,
Teas
and
Rambling
Parties.

School
Treats
a
Speciality.

10
minutes'
walk
from
Chingford
Station.

Opened in July 1888, the Royal Epping Forest Golf Club's course on Chingford Plain was the first public course in Essex. Elaborate measures were required to avoid hitting stray day-trippers who frequently wandered across the course. At one stage, July and August were treated as a close season due to the press of visitors, while at another time, players had to wear scarlet tunics on the green to enure they were visible!

Larkswood Pool, shortly after its opening in 1936, was regarded as one of the best open-air pools ever constructed.

This view of Larkswood Pool dates from around 1960.

THE AVENUE, CHINGFORD.

Boys have gathered round the water trough at the junction of Bury Road and Rangers Road, known as The Avenue along this section, in 1900. Note the horse-brakes lined up beyond.

Boating on Connaught Water was a popular pastime in 1905...

...and in 1917.

If the weather was inclement, what about a visit to the cinema? Opening as the Chingford Pavilion on 14 October 1920, it changed its name to the Chingford Cinema in 1930, becoming the Doric in 1941. It survived until the 1960s; an office block now stands on the site. There was also a large Odeon (later Classic) in Cherrydown Avenue; after closure in 1972 a supermarket now stands on the site.

Larks Wood is an ancient fragment of woodland which survived the development of the southern part of Chingford. In 1936, what remained of the wood was included in Larkswood Park, which was then opened to the public; at forty-seven acres this is Chingford's largest park.

Mansfield Park, c. 1960. Chingford's parks and allotments comprise some 200 acres. The name Mansfield, also seen in Mansfield Hill, derives from the Anglo-Saxon gemæne, meaning land held in common. The area originally consisted of Leaside marsh which was used for communal grazing and hay-cropping.

Ridgeway Park, c. 1960. A pleasant scene with children fishing for 'tiddlers'.

Cycling down 'Little Church Hill', that section of Old Church Road above the old church. Cycling was an immensely popular leisure activity at the end of the nineteenth century and before the First World War, and cycle meets, often in fancy dress, were a regular feature of Chingford life.

This 0-6-0 loco, No. 2715, is the 9.55 a.m. excursion train leaving Chingford station for Southend-on-Sea.

When all other forms of entertainment failed, Chingford residents could always rise to the occasion by putting on their own amusements. Here a group of ladies are dancing outside the Fountain public house, c. 1897.

Five

Chingford People

Above: Thomas Boothby (1549–1625), a merchant tailor from London, began the long association of the Boothby family with Chingford. In 1608 he bought the manor of Chingford Earls, and the Boothby family remained as lords of the manor until 1774, when it passed to the Heathcotes. The Heathcotes then held the manor until the death of Louisa Boothby Heathcote in 1940.

Left: Dick Turpin (1705–1739), the notorious highwayman and his gang of muggers and burglars was active in the Epping Forest area; his men robbed the house of one John Gladwin on Chingford Green in 1734, and he himself hid out at Sewardstone, just north of Chingford, on several occasions.

Teachers at Chingford National School, *c*. 1880. The National School was Chingford's earliest; it was in existence by 1817, and survives to this day as Chingford Church of England Junior School.

A posse of likely lads take a rest from their exertions on Chingford Mount Road, *c.* 1892.

Left: Some of Chingford's volunteer firemen stand proudly in front of a bonfire they built to celebrate Queen Victoria's Diamond Jubilee in 1897.

Below: Volunteer firemen again, here seen in action putting out the 1912 fire at the Royal Forest Hotel.

Opposite above: More firemen, resplendent in their uniforms, *c.* 1930. They have clearly been awarded a silver shield, but the event is otherwise unknown.

Opposite below: Chingford firemen pose beside their tender, *c.* 1930.

Staff line up on Chingford station platform. The 1891 census recorded a stationmaster, refreshment manageress, barmaid, servant, 6 railway clerks, 1 ticket collector, 2 signalmen, foreman porter and 7 porters, and 4 platelayers working for the Great Eastern Railway.

A Chingford bobby looks on, around 1905, while a group of lady cyclists are waiting outside Chingford station.

Right: Walthamstow U.D.C. tramways staff pose in their open-top tram at Chingford Mount. From 1905, Walthamstow Council ran a service from the Bakers Arms to Chingford Mount.

Below: Posing on Flanders Weir, *c.* 1885. Are these people fishermen, the lock-keeper and friends, or just passers-by? Flanders Weir on the Lea now lies beneath the William Girling Reservoir, completed in 1951.

Chingford's policemen pose outside their newly completed station on Kings Head Hill.

Chingford police again, this time out of uniform and photographed during a local cricket match against a village side. The old Bull & Crown can be seen on the far left of the picture.

Above: The landlord of the Queen Elizabeth hotel, Forest Side, poses proudly outside his inn, *c.* 1890.

Right: Three children are lost in thought amid the ruins of Chingford old church. Part of the nave roof collapsed in 1904 and the building was not restored until 1928–30.

The ladies pose outside Inks Green Farm, *c.* 1910, which stood on Hale End Road (now Larkshall Road) at the entrance to Larks Wood. The farm was later known as Roper's Farm after the family who lived there, but this photo may show members of their predecessors, the Sutton family. The farm was demolished around 1960.

The weather is too bracing to go out on Connaught Water, so these boatmen are left with their thoughts and their dog, and a melancholy line of unhired canoes.

Right: A striking figure of a man; this is Robert Boothby Heathcote, lord of the manor of Chingford Earls from 1838 and rector from 1829–65. He owned 600 acres of prime Chingford land, mainly around Friday Hill and Pimp Hall. His daughter Louisa died at a great age in 1940 and thereafter the estate was bought by the London County Council for development.

Below: Fun at a fancy dress Chingford cycle meet. Here a couple of chaps from East Ham have pre-empted The Flintstones!

Above: Robert Donat starred in the original version of *Goodbye Mr Chips*. The novel itself was written by James Hilton (1900–55), who spent his childhood at Brookfield House, Hale End, and based the work on the life of his own father, a local schoolmaster.

Below: T.E. Lawrence (1888–1935) bought land on Pole Hill, hoping to build a permanent home there. He also wanted to print *The Seven Pillars of Wisdom* in huts on the hill. He later sold the land to Chingford Council.

Opposite above: Stunned local residents pick over the ruins of houses in Endlebury Road after a V-2 attack on 5 February 1945. Eleven V-2 rockets and eleven V-1 flying bombs fell on the borough, and hundreds of lesser bombs. A total of 11,166 properties (out of a total of 11,275 in the borough) received some form of damage during the Second World War.

Opposite below: An emergency feeding centre set up on Kings Head Hill after the Endelbury Road incident. A total of eighty-nine residents lost their lives through bombing during the war.

Winston Churchill addressing an election rally on 3 July 1945 at Walthamstow Stadium, just outside the Chingford boundary. Churchill represented the district as MP for many years.

Six

South Chingford
and Chingford Mount

The original Saxon settlement of Chingford probably lay in the south-west of the parish in the area of Cook's Ferry. The low-lying marshes of the Lea were crossed by the Eastern Counties Railway in 1837 by a viaduct from Stratford.

The rural peace of the Lea before development is captured in this 1907 postcard.

Much of the Lea valley is under water now, the marshes and meanders lying beneath the King George's reservoir, which was begun in 1908 and completed in 1913, and the William Girling reservoir, begun in 1935 and opened in 1951. This view shows part of the interior of the pumping station of King George's reservoir, which has a capacity of 2,729 million gallons.

Chingford's ancient parish church dates from the twelfth century, with later additions. It was originally dedicated to All Saints, though by 1710 it was known as St Peter and St Paul. When the new church was built on Chingford Green in 1844, it was dedicated to St Peter and St Paul, so the old church reverted to its original name of All Saints. It was however usually known locally as the 'old church' or the 'green church', as it was so covered with ivy and moss.

Chingford old church was always isolated from the centre of population, and as Chingford Green developed it became even more remote. The tower was built at the beginning of the fifteenth century and soon after there were extensive alterations which brought the church to something like its present appearance.

Chingford old church, c. 1900. After the opening of the new church, All Saints was largely abandoned and suffered several thefts and much weathering. By 1900 it was largely ruinous and completely ivy-clad.

Above: In 1904 part of the roof nave collapsed, and the broken church became something of a tourist attraction. It was restored by the architect Charles Winmill in 1928-30, the cost of the work – some £6,000 – being paid for by Louisa Heathcote.

Right: Chingford old church gave rise to at least one ghost story. The tale of the Chingford miser and his fate after his death is wryly told in the anonymous poem The Miser published in 1901.

THE MISER

(Legend of Chingford Old Church).

N a lonely hill (with grass o'ergrown),
   Surrounded by meadows green,
   Standing alone, all ivy-grown,
    Old Chingford Church is seen.

The ivy around its tower doth creep
  As time onward stealthily crawls ;
Lone watch it doth keep over those that sleep
  Around its crumbling walls.

     *   *   *   *

A long time ago, the story is told
  Of a miser who lived near here,
Who, wicked and old, had hoarded his gold
  Greedily year after year.

Chingford Hall. The manor house of Chingford St Paul's was built in the early nineteenth century, replacing a sixteenth-century building, and stood in what is now a triangle of roads formed by the North Circular Road, Hall Lane and Lower Hall Lane. The site is now entirely industrial.

A muddy day, c. 1905 outside the Prince Albert as a tram bound for Lea Bridge Road passes a heavily laden wagon.

Another view of 'Prince Albert Corner', *c.* 1905. Passers-by have stopped to watch the tram, then a novelty in Chingford. When the service began, there were mixed feelings about bringing trams to Chingford. The local newspaper reported, 'the trams of Walthamstow seem to please some people and to annoy others'.

The Prince Albert. The core of the building still exists but is completely obscured by modern shops.

Three advertisements for local tradesmen in South Chingford; Hardwick's advert dates from 1931, the others from 1949.

Old Church Road, looking south-west towards Hall Lane, *c.* 1930. Fairs were occasionally held on the open ground to the right.

A similar view a few years later; the open ground has been turned into a small green and some of the houses have become shops.

The same 'green' looking in the opposite direction.

During the Second World War, the 'green' was converted into a Civil Defence wardens' post. Note the Chingford Odeon behind; this was an original Oscar Deutsch Odeon, designed by Andrew Mather, and could seat over 1,200 people in its cavernous auditorium.

'Prince Albert Corner', *c.* 1950.

A busy street scene at 'Prince Albert Corner' at the same time.

South Chingford library, Hall Lane, opened in the 1930s, designed in a very severe architectural style.

South Chingford library; an interior view from the 1930s.

Old Church Road in around 1905. Chingford old church, with fallen roof, is at the top of the hill, and the white weatherboarded Cherrydown Farm can be seen below it on the left.

The same view in 1926.

Left: Cherrydown Farm in 1930. This farm stood halfway up Old Church Road. The name has nothing to do with cherries but derives from Anglo-Saxon cirice meaning 'church'; All Saints church stood very close by.

Below: Old Church Road, *c.* 1910, close to the entrance to Chingford Mount Cemetery.

CHINGFORD MOUNT

J. CUSWORTH & SONS

Chingford Mount Cemetery was opened in 1884 by the Abney Park Cemetery Company. Many notable and notorious people lie buried there; one of the largest funerals to take place at the cemetery in recent years was the burial in 1995 of East End gangster, Ronnie Kray.

The entrance gates to Chingford Mount Cemetery. The cemetery was laid out on the grounds of an earlier property, Caroline House.

A snowy scene looking back down Chingford Mount in January 1968.

Thirsty travellers reaching the top of Old Church Road have always been able to refresh themselves at the Green Man public house.

Seven

Chingford Hatch

Left: The Ching forms the eastern boundary of Chingford. Its original name seems to have been the Bourne. This idyllic postcard dates from 1906.

Below: The hamlet of Hale End, seen here around 1905, straddled the Chingford–Walthamstow boundary. Following the opening of the station at Highams Park, the name Hale End fell out of use, and the subsequent estate which developed was known as Highams Park.

The original station at Highams Park (which lies in Walthamstow) was opened in 1873 and rebuilt in 1900.

The Avenue, Highams Park, *c.* 1910, with Highams Park station in the background.

The Dun Cow in Hatch Lane, *c.* 1905; a very rural scene.

The Dun Cow was later replaced by the Manor Hotel, seen here with the Ching bridge in the foreground.

The Manor Hotel was itself replaced in 1971 by a new roundabout and pub, the Horseless Carriage, now known as 'Wheelwrights Restaurant'.

Larks Hall Farm, c. 1910. This was one of Chingford's last working farms. It was in the hands of the McCunn family until the 1970s, when it was taken over for use as a home for one-parent families. After being threatened with demolition it was finally, in 1982, converted into a public house, the Larkshall.

Chingford Hatch level crossing from Larkhall Road, c. 1885.

A more recent view of the level crossing, dating from 1971, shortly before an underpass obviated the need for the gates.

The Wesleyan chapel in Hatch Lane was built in 1862. This photograph dates from 1906 or 1907.

This footpath led from Hale End to Ainslie Wood Road. Playing fields for staff of the local Caribonum Works were later laid out on this site.

No. 1 Newgate Street, Chingford Hatch – Old Farm stood opposite this fine old building.

The Prince of Wales inn.

Friday Hill in 1938, looking north from the River Ching.

Friday Hill House. This was home of the Boothbys and later the Heathcotes. Robert Boothby Heathcote had the old seventeenth-century house pulled down and rebuilt in a grand style in 1839; the architect was Vulliamy, who also designed the new parish church on Chingford Green.

Friday Hill House. After the death of Louisa Boothby Heathcote in 1940 and the subsequent development of the Friday Hill estate, the house was turned into a community centre. According to tradition it was here (or perhaps at Pimp Hall) that King James I once jokingly knighted a piece of beef, dubbing it 'Sir Loin' after a day's hunting in the Forest.

Friday Hill, looking towards Little Friday Hill House. This house has recently been converted into a pub, the Sir Loin.

A view from around 1890 of fields looking north-west towards Larks Wood. The lane in the foreground is now Castle Avenue, Highams Park, and the area beyond the railway line (in the middle distance) is now covered by the Warboys estate.

Another view of fields, this time from Friday Hill, looking north-east before the development of the L.C.C. estate.

After the war, the Friday Hill estate sprang up on those fields. Here we see newly-built council houses in Winslow Grove.

Pimp hall in the 1890s – a farm worker poses with his spade. This building began life as the manor house of the manor of 'Gowers and Buckerells', a name dating back to the thirteenth century. The name Pimp Hall derives from one Reynold Pympe, who lived some two centuries later.

Pimp Hall remained a working farm until 1934, when it was bought by Chingford Council and the grounds were converted into a nursery and allotments. The Bolton family were the last tenant farmers. The farm itself was a timber-framed structure of the sixteenth century.

Pimp Hall Farm was demolished 1936–9, with the exception of an historic seventeenth-century barn and dovecote.

Hatch Lane, c. 1960. The word 'hatch' derives from the Anglo-Saxon word hæcc, meaning 'gate' or 'gateway', usually, as in this case, with reference to a gate across a track into the Forest.

Another view of Hatch Lane at the same time.

Eight

Chingford –
Suburban Dream

Long View Old Church Hill, South Chingford

In many ways, Chingford embodies the suburban dream; a civilised place to live, with plenty of amenities, a rich social life, close to the countryside yet also convenient for London. The photographs and advertisements in this final section are a random selection of views illustrating the development of Chingford as a suburban dream town. This view shows the solid interwar terraces of Old Church Road.

Bass houses advertised in 1927.

The pleasant terraces of Chingford Road in the days before the car became king. This view looks south to the junction of Sinclair and Ainslie Wood Roads.

The delightfully named Dingley Dell estate promoted in this 1935 advert.

Long Deacon Road, c. 1926 – everyone's idea of the ideal 'semi'.

Chas. Hare's advert in 1927.

Art Deco style houses in Mansfield Hill.

Hennah's advert, 1935.

A rather rural-looking New Road, before 'improvement' in 1931.

New Road after 1931, 'improved' by new road surfacing, pavements, and more housing!

The Mount Echo estate, advertised in 1935.

The Endlebury estate under construction, 1930.

Building work proceeds on the Endlebury estate, seen here from the junction of Larkshall and Endlebury Roads.

After the completion of the Endlebury estate, 1936.

66

Larkshall Road in 1937.

Peachey builders – and estate agents – advertise in 1935.

Friday Hill, 29 September 1955. The open road beckons.